THE
ASSYRIAN INVASIONS
AND DEPORTATIONS
OF ISRAEL

By

J. LLEWELLYN THOⅠ

Author of
"God and my Birthright,"; "The Restoration of Israel";
"Israel and the Church,"; "The Abrahamic and Mosaic Covenants"
and "Fulfilment of Covenant Promises"

A REPRINT OF 1937 EDITION BY
COVENANT PUBLISHING COMPANY, BRITAIN

PUBLISHED BY

ARTISAN SALES
P.O. BOX 1497, THOUSAND OAKS
CALIF. 91360 U.S.A.

ISBN: 0-934666-33-4

1

PREFACE TO U.S. EDITION

During the some fifty years since J. Llewellyn Thomas wrote 'The Assyrian Invasions and Deportations of Israel' opponents of the Israel-Identity Truth continue to produce the same outworn and fallacious arguments in opposition to the facts. Thomas largely based his conclusions on the Scriptures and ancient inscriptions found on Assyrian monuments. However, his scholarship and research has in recent years been incontestably corroborated by the testimony of the clay cuneiform tablets found (in 1850 A.D.) at Nineveh, in the Assyrian Royal Library of Ashurbanipal.

The cuneiform tablets, known as the 'Royal Correspondence of the Assyrian Empire' provided the 'links' between the so-called 'Lost Tribes of Israel' and the Scythians and Cimmerians from whom most of the caucasian inhabitants of Western Europe, Scandinavia, Britain and America are descended. At the time of their translation in 1930, the relevence of the tablets to Israel was overlooked because they were in complete disorder and among hundreds of miscellaneous texts dealing with many matters of state. Contributing to this situation was the fact that the Assyrians called the Israelites by other names during their captivity.

For the complete story of the tablets, together with photos and translations, the publisher is pleased to offer the publication, 'Missing Links Discovered in Assyrian Tablets' by E. Raymond Capt – Artisan Sales 1985. See listing on inside rear cover.

CONTENTS

TABLES

3

ACKNOWLEDGEMENT

We wish to thank the Covenant Publishing Company of London, Britain for their permission to publish the U.S. edition of their work.

The Publisher - Artisan Sales
January, 1989

INTRODUCTION TO THE ASSYRIAN INVASIONS

CONTENTS

The Question at Issue.
    Contrary Views as to the Extent of the Deportations.
    Appeal to the Scriptures.

The Difference between II Kings and II Chronicles.

Ezra, the Great Editor.

Sources of our Knowledge of the Deportations.
    (1) "The Book of the Chronicles of the Kings of Israel."
    (2) "The Book of the Chronicles of the Kings of Judah."

A. The Scriptures.
    The Second Book of Kings.
    The First Book of Chronicles.
    The Prophetic Writings of Hosea, Isaiah and Jeremiah.

B. The Monuments:
    The Inscriptions of the Assyrian Kings.

The Assyrian Invasions of Israel.
    In the Reigns of Menahem, Pekah and Hoshea.
    By the Emperors Pul, Tiglath-pileser, Shalmaneser and Sargon.
    Four Narratives of Three Invasions.

INTRODUCTION TO THE ASSYRIAN INVASIONS

DEFINITE statements on the subject of the Deportation of the Israelites of the Northern Kingdom from Palestine into Assyria have been made by some eminent authorities of the Church of England.

They deny that Israel was ever entirely carried away into captivity and state that the whole nation was never removed out of their land.

They assert that those of the captivity were quite insignificant in number, that the bulk of the nation remained in their land long after the invasions.

Others hold that it can be demonstrated from Scripture that the entire nation of the Ten Tribes was carried away out of Palestine into Assyria.

The question at issue is of great importance, and must be settled by reference to the Holy Scriptures, the final Court of Appeal in all such matters.

The histories of the kingdoms of Israel and of Judah were severally recorded in each kingdom by its State Recorders. As we read through the Second Book of Kings we note that after the death of each king it is stated that the events are recorded "in the book of the chronicles of the kings of" Israel or Judah as the case may be. These separate national chronicles are not to be confused with the First and Second Book of Chronicles of our Bible.

When the kingdom ceased to exist these State Chronicles naturally came to an end. Any record of subsequent events must of necessity be by other hands, some scribe, priest or prophet; but the State Record ceased.

THE Second Book of Chronicles deals solely with the history of the kingdom of Judah, and has nothing to do with the history of Israel, save where it affected Judah, and thus comes into the history of Judah.

The Second Book of Kings on the other hand is the history of both kingdoms. It is a combination of two separate histories, excerpts from the records of the two kingdoms. It gives an account of the reign of each several king in one section; a mosaic of the different reigns in more or less chronological order.

EZRA THE GREAT EDITOR

It seems generally agreed that Ezra the great scribe and priest, who returned to Judea with the small portion of the captives of Judah from Babylon after the seventy years, was the editor who compiled these two separate histories into the one history as we have it in our Bible as the Second Book of Kings. This he is supposed to have accomplished probably before 536 B.C., that is during the Judah captivity in Babylon.

The task of an inspired editor to make a single history out of the State Records of two separate nations would not be an easy one. He might have re-written the whole *de novo* in strict chronological order of events; but this would not have been exactly the work of an editor. The work rather consisted in piecing together the portions of the old records, without alteration, but with an opportunity of adding editorial remarks to elucidate the original texts, and of finishing off the story by the addition of much later events bearing on the subject, and of giving a review of the history.

Thus a record of the entire reign of one king is given, and then the entire history of a contemporary or subsequent king of the other kingdom; and this even when the events of the two reigns took place at the same date. In this way the events of a second section did not necessarily happen at the end of the previous section but at some earlier date. The ordinary reader might well think that the second section was a strict continuation (in point of time) of the previous one. In other words the *events* are not necessarily arranged in exact chronological order though the reigns are.

For example the reigns of Hoshea king of Israel and of Hezekiah king of Judah as narrated in II Kings xvi and xvii were to a certain extent contemporary, yet the complete history of Hoshea is given before the history of Hezekiah begins. This leads one to conclude that all the doings of Hezekiah's reign began after the end of Hoshea's reign, whereas the early events of Hezekiah's reign happened when Hoshea ruled over the kingdom of Israel. Not to grasp this simple fact is to misunderstand the true history of that period. Care is needed to note the chronological order of the events. To this we refer later.

SOURCES OF OUR KNOWLEDGE OF THE INVASIONS AND DEPORTATIONS

The accounts of the Assyrian invasions are gained in the main from the Scriptures, and also from the Assyrian Inscriptions of that period.

I. THE SCRIPTURE INFORMATION.

(a) This is mainly recorded in the Second Book of Kings under the headings of "the book of the chronicles of the kings of Israel," in Chapters xv, xvi and xvii.

(b) There are references to the fall of Samaria and to Israel in "the book of the chronicles of the kings of Judah" found in II Kings.

(c) The First Book of Chronicles gives an account of one of the invasions.

(d) The prophets Hosea and Isaiah prophesied about Israel's captivity: while Jeremiah gave information of the position of Israel in his day.

All these passages will be considered in due course.

II. THE TESTIMONY OF THE MONUMENTS

Apart from the Bible there are Assyrian inscriptions concerning the invasions and deportations of Israel by the Assyrian kings. These cuneiform inscriptions may be seen in the British Museum, and will be touched upon: they only confirm the Scriptures and in no way contradict them.

The Assyrian Invasions of Israel all occurred in the time of Israel's last four kings, and culminated in the destruction of the kingdom.

The story of the later kings of Israel is one of conspiracy, assassination and usurpation. King Shallum had murdered his predecessor Zechariah, the last king of Jehu's dynasty; but he enjoyed his illgotten throne for but one month before he himself was assassinated by Menahem. This king held the royal power for ten years, and was succeeded by his son Pekahiah, who after a short reign of two years was murdered by Pekah. Pekah after he had reigned for twenty years was murdered by Hoshea, who was the last of Israel's kings in the Holy Land.

The invasions took place in the reigns of:

> Menahem.
> Pekah.
> Hoshea.

There was no invasion during Pekahiah's short reign.

The Bible gives four accounts of these invasions. Three of them are found in the Second Book of Kings:

> II Kings xv, 19-20.
> II Kings xv, 29.
> II Kings xvii, 3-6.

and one in the First Book of Chronicles:

> I Chronicles v, 26.

The latter is another account of the one mentioned in II Kings xv, 29. Thus we have in all, four accounts of three invasions.

The names of the invading Emperors given in these passages are:

> Pul.
> Tiglath-pileser.
> Shalmaneser.

Pul was the same person as Tiglath-pileser, he assumed the name which was that of a famous previous emperor. (See the Encyclopaedia Britannica.)

The Bible does not mention Sargon by name in this connection: we learn however from secular history that he was the "tartan" of Shalmaneser's forces, and that he seized the throne upon the death of Shalmaneser, which occurred towards the end of the siege of Samaria; and that it was actually he who effected the capture of the city. This fact would be unknown to the Recorder of the Israel chronicles within the beleaguered city, as he does not mention the fact.

We now proceed to study these invasions.

THE FIRST AND SECOND INVASIONS

CONTENTS

Two Notable Prophecies:
1. Hosea, (a) The Jezreel Prophecy.
   (b) The Lo-Ruhamah Prophecy.
2. Isaiah, The Three Score and Five Years Prophecy.

The First Invasion.
In the reign of Menahem.
By Pul alias Tiglath-pileser.
No Territory Annexed. No Captives Carried Away.

The Second Invasion.
In the Reign of Pekah.
By Pul alias Tiglath-pileser.
Causes of the Invasion.
Extent of the Conquest.
Assyrian Annexation of the Conquered Territory.
Deportation of Captives.
Location of the Captives in Assyria.
Parallel Account in Chronicles.
The Assassination of Pekah.
Hoshea Recognised as King by Assyria.
Annual Tribute Imposed.
Assyrian Inscriptions of this Invasion.

THE FIRST AND SECOND INVASIONS

AMONG the several prophecies foretelling the Captivity of Israel, two notable prophecies demand special attention. They were made by Hosea and Isaiah.

HOSEA'S PROPHECIES

(a) *The First* was uttered on the birth of his firstborn son Jezreel:

> "And the Lord said unto him, Call his name Jezreel; for yet a little while, and I will avenge the blood of Jezreel upon the house of Jehu, and *will cause to cease the kingdom of the house of Israel*" (Hos. i, 4).

(b) *The Second* was uttered on the birth of his only daughter Lo-Ruhamah :

> "And God said unto him, Call her name Lo-Ruhamah; for I will no more have mercy upon the house of Israel; but *I will utterly take them away*" (Hos. i, 6).

The First speaks of the Fall of the Kingdom.
The Second speaks of the Deportation of the Nation.
No fixable dates are given for these events. It is evident that the two events were not to be synchronous; the nation is not to be carried utterly away at the time of the fall of the kingdom.

ISAIAH'S PROPHECY

This was spoken when Pekah king of Israel with Rezin king of Syria contemplated attacking Ahaz king of Judah.

> "Within three score and five years shall Ephraim be broken *that it be not a people*" (Isa. vii, 8).

12

Here, fortunately, we are able to fix approximate dates, for these words were uttered just before 741 B.C. And we are told that within sixty-five years Israel would be broken so that it would be no longer "a People," obviously a People in Palestine.

It says nothing about the cessation of the Kingdom in the land, but only of the cessation of the Nation there.

Hosea's Lo-Ruhamah prophecy and Isaiah's Three Score and Five Years prophecy describe the same event; they are synchronous and refer to a complete transportation of the entire nation from Palestine.

Sixty-five years from 741 would be about 676 B.C., a crucial date in the history of Israel and one to be borne in mind.

THE FIRST INVASION

As already stated the first invasion was by Pul, Tiglath-pileser in the reign of Menahem (II Kings xv, 19-20). Only the northern outskirts of Israel's land were invaded, when Menahem bought off the king of Assyria with a huge ransom of four thousand pounds of silver. Tiglath-pileser thereupon retired, having taken possession of no territory, and having carried away no captives with him.

This first invasion was therefore but a light affliction as compared with what was to follow later. It is usually ignored and not reckoned an invasion at all since it left the kingdom intact as before.

The Bible account is as follows:

> "And Pul the king of Assyria came against the land; and Menahem gave Pul a thousand talents of silver, that his hand might be with him to confirm the kingdom in his hand. And Menahem exacted the money from Israel, even of all the mighty men of wealth, of each fifty shekels of silver, to give to the king of Assyria. So the king of Assyria turned back, and stayed not there in the land" (II Kings xv, 19-20).

THE SECOND INVASION

The Second invasion is recorded in II Kings xv, 29. This occurred in the reign of Pekah, and was prosecuted by Tiglath-pileser.

13

Here is the record :

"In the days of Pekah king of Israel came Tiglath-pileser king of Assyria, and took Ijon, and Abel-beth-maachah, and Janoah, and Kadesh, and Hazor, and Gilead, and Galilee, all the land of Naphtali, and carried them captive to Assyria.

And Hoshea the son of Elah made a conspiracy against Pekah the son of Remaliah, and smote him, and slew him, and reigned in his stead" (II Kings xv, 20).

CAUSES OF THE INVASION

What were the circumstances that led up to this invasion? Towards the end of his reign Pekah in alliance with Rezin, king of Syria, made an attack upon Judah, II Kings xv, 37, xvi, 5, and Isa. vii, 2. Ahaz had succeeded to the throne of Judah on the death of his father Jotham. These allied kings for some reason conceived the idea of conquering Judah, of dethroning the new king Ahaz, and of setting the son of Tabeal on the throne of Judah.

It was at this time that the term "Jews" first appears in the Bible, II Kings, xvi, 6. It covered all the people of the kingdom of Judah, composed of the tribes of Judah and Benjamin and all the Levites, and no other tribes. The next mention of the name "Jew" occurs in the reign of Hezekiah (son of Ahaz), when Sennacherib (son of Sargon) invaded Judah (II Kings xviii, 26 and 28).

The prophet Isaiah assured king Ahaz that the project of these allied kings, whom he designated as "these smoking firebrands," would not succeed. It was on this occasion that he uttered the notable prophecy against Israel, stating the time of her downfall.

"Within three score and five years shall Ephraim be broken that it be not a people" (Isa. vii, 8).

Ahaz, in spite of the prophet's assurance that the purpose of the two kings should not stand or come to pass, was thoroughly alarmed, and called in Tiglath-pileser to his assistance (II Kings xvi, 7). He humbled himself exceedingly and sent to the Assyrians all the gold and silver on which he could lay hands.

14

Tiglath-pileser thereupon marshalled his forces against Syria and Israel. He conquered Syria and slew Rezin, and then turned upon Israel.

His campaign is clearly outlined in the above account. He invaded the northern region of the land, coming down south to the level of the Sea of Galilee, where he turned eastwards and invaded the eastern portion of Israel, Transjordania, which reached southward nearly to the level of the Dead Sea. This was the extent of the second invasion of Israel. The date of it was 741 B.C. The adjoining map shows the territory invaded and annexed.

It is noteworthy that the tribe of Dan is never mentioned in these accounts whilst the other tribes are named. The northern Danites should have been the first to feel the Assyrian impact. They were not there, and are believed to have migrated by sea to avoid the foreseen Assyrian menace.

The Deportation of Captives

Now occurred the first deportation of Israel from the conquered regions. The number of the captives taken is not mentioned. They were removed "to Assyria": their exact location is not told us in this account, but from the parallel narrative in I Chronicles we find that it was to the same regions where the subsequent deportations were settled, namely, Hala, Habor, Hara and the river Gozan. It must have been a great host for the Assyrian king in his Inscriptions says: "*All of its people* together with their goods I carried off to Assyria." (See below.)

The Parallel Account of the Second Invasion

Another account of this invasion is found in I Chronicle v, 26.

"And the God of Israel stirred up the spirit of Pul, king of Assyria, and the spirit of Tiglath-pileser, king of Assyria, and *he* carried them away, even the Reubenites, and the Gadites and the half tribe of Manasseh, and brought them unto Hala, and Habor, and Hara and to the river Gozan, unto this day."

From this account it might appear that the invasion was by

15

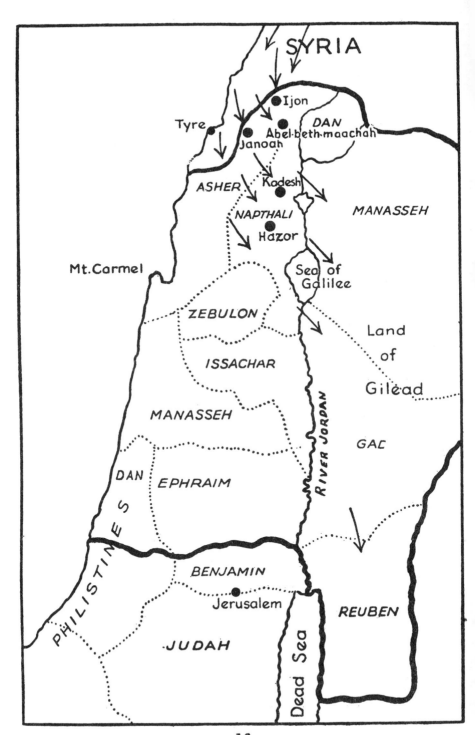

SYRIA

Ijon

Tyre

DAN

Abel-beth-maachah

Janoah

ASHER

Kadesh

MANASSEH

NAPTHALI

Hazor

Mt. Carmel

Sea of Galilee

ZEBULON

Land

ISSACHAR

of

Gilead

MANASSEH

RIVER JORDAN

GAD

DAN

EPHRAIM

PHILISTINES

BENJAMIN

Jerusalem

REUBEN

Dead Sea

JUDAH

two separate kings; but it adds that *"he* carried them away," showing that they were one and the same person. As mentioned above Pul assumed the second name.

This narrative mentions no number of the captives, but their precise location in Assyria is given. It also states that they were there "unto this day," indicating that at the time of writing the Book of Chronicles, which was long years after this event, these captives had not returned to Judea with the partial return of the Jews from their captivity in Babylon as some would fain have us believe.

In these first two invasions of Israel were fulfilled Isaiah's words:

> "Nevertheless the dimness shall not be such as was in her vexation, when at the first He lightly afflicted the land of Zebulun and the land of Naphtali (the first invasion) and afterwards did more grievously afflict her by the way of the sea, beyond Jordan, in Galilee of the nations" (the second invasion) (Isa. ix, 1).

At the end of this invasion, Pekah, king of Israel, was murdered by Hoshea, who seized the throne. Hoshea was recognised as the lawful king by Tiglath-pileser, and was made to pay tribute to the Assyrians.

ASSYRIAN INSCRIPTIONS CONCERNING THE SECOND INVASION

In "The Ancient Records of Assyria and Babylon," by D. D. Luckenbill, p. 292, there are two inscriptions given of the invasion:

> "The cities of . . . Gala'za, Abilkka, which are on the border of Bit-Humria . . . the whole land of Naphtali, in its entirety, I brought within the border of Assyria. My official I set over them as governor . . . "

And again:

> "The land of Bit-Humria . . . all of its people together with all their goods I carried off to Assyria. Pakaha their king they deposed, and I placed Ausi as king. Ten talents

17

of gold, ten talents of silver, as their tribute I received from them, and to Assyria I carried them."

Pakaha was the Assyrian for Pekah, and Ausi for Hoshea.

These inscriptions are of value because they completely corroborate the statements of God's Word.

It will be seen from the map that the territory of the kingdom of Israel was thus reduced to a third of its original size.

It is obvious that neither the Jezreel nor the Lo-Ruhamah prophecies of Hosea were fulfilled at this time: nor was Isaiah's Three Score and Five Years prophecy fulfilled now, in fact it had only just been uttered.

THE THIRD INVASION

CONTENTS

THE THIRD INVASION

The Third Invasion of Israel was by the Emperor Shalmaneser, whose commander-in-chief was Sargon. It took place in the sixth year of Hoshea.

There are some who suggest that Shalmaneser made two invasions. The first of these mentioned in II Kings xvii, 3, where it says:

> "Against him came up Shalmaneser, king of Assyria, and Hoshea became his servant, and gave him presents."

The second in verse 5 of the same chapter:

> "Then the king of Assyria came up throughout all the land, and went up to Samaria and besieged it three years."

Whatever the truth may be concerning this point, it is the so-called second one that is of supreme importance, and the first is ignored by all, and both are generally regarded as only one.

This Third Invasion was most disastrous, for it terminated the kingdom of Israel in Palestine. Here is the whole account of it:

> "Against him came up Shalmaneser, king of Assyria; and Hoshea became his servant, and gave him presents. And the king of Assyria found conspiracy in Hoshea: for he had sent messengers to So, king of Egypt, and brought no present to the king of Assyria, as he had done year by year: therefore the king of Assyria shut him up, and bound him in prison. Then the king of Assyria came up throughout all the land, and went up to Samaria, and besieged it three years" (II Kings xvii, 3 to 5).

This campaign began about 723 B.C., and ended in 721.

The refusal of Hoshea to continue to pay to Shalmaneser the annual tribute exacted by Assyria was the cause of this invasion; and to this was added the fact that Hoshea had appealed to Egypt for assistance; a very serious matter for Assyrian ambitions and foreign policy. Shalmaneser somehow made Hoshea a prisoner, and began hostilities. He overran the land and laid siege to the capital. It is strange to realise that during this campaign the king of Israel was a prisoner in the hands of the enemy. Whether other cities were taken, and captives carried away is not recorded in the Bible; such events would not be known to the State Recorder shut up in the beleaguered capital. There are no monumental records of the campaign by Shalmaneser extant. It is said that all such, if any, were destroyed by Sargon: but this is not relevant to our subject.

Sayce in his great book, "Assyria, its Princes, Priests and People," p. 48, shows that Shalmaneser died, or was murdered, a year before Samaria fell, and that it was Sargon who actually completed its reduction. This fact is not recorded in the Bible for the simple reason that the State Recorder of Israel, shut up in Samaria, would not have been aware of such events, and would have had no opportunity of writing them after the fall of the city, because he, with all the officials and inhabitants, was carried away captive to Assyria. For the same reason he could not have recorded the actual fall of the city, or state the number of the captives carried away into Assyria, or their location in that land. All such information must come from other sources.

THE DEPORTATION, THE ORTHODOX VIEW

From reading the xvii Chapter of II Kings, it has been universally understood (1) that the Israelites were all deported after the fall of Samaria to Assyria:

(2) that the entire nation was then removed out of God's sight because it states that only Judah was left behind in the land:

(3) that Shalmaneser was the Assyrian king who performed this wholesale deportation:

(4) that it was Shalmaneser who brought in all the various Gentile tribes mentioned in verse 24 to repopulate the land thus denuded of Israelites.

Objections to the Orthodox View

These points need careful examination. Against these commonly held views there are several adverse considerations.

A. If Israel was indeed entirely removed from the land upon the fall of Samaria, "the Three Score and Five Years" prophecy by Isaiah entirely failed and was not true. In 721, B.C. when Samaria fell, only twenty of the sixty-five years had elapsed, there were yet another forty-five to run before "Ephraim shall be broken that it be not a people." Hence it is evident that Israel at this time was not entirely cast out of Palestine.

B. Shalmaneser could not have been the Assyrian king who effected the wholesale deportation of Israel. He, as we have seen, died in the third year of the siege, he did not live to see the end of the invasion or to return to Assyria. It seems impossible that he carried away any captives at all.

C. Much less could he have brought in those Gentile hordes into the land of Israel. The Bible does not tell who "the king of Assyria" was who did this filling of the land with these aliens. It has been presumed that it was the king whose name is last mentioned in the chapter, namely Shalmaneser, but this is a gratuitous assumption without foundation.

In all fairness it should here be mentioned that Josephus states that it was Shalmaneser who did all this. In his "Antiquities" Book ix and Chapter xiii, he writes:

> "This conquest proved wholly destructive of the kingdom of Israel, Hoshea being made a prisoner, and his subjects being transplanted to Media in Persia, and replaced by people whom *Shalmaneser* caused to be removed from the borders of Chuthah, a river in Persia for setting in the land of Samaria."

Shalmaneser, had he not died, could not have moved Israel into Media, because Media at that time did not belong to the Assyrian empire: it was only conquered and taken by Assyria some years later, whereupon many of the Israel captives were removed thither as attested by the inscriptions of Sargon.

Josephus takes the prevalent view and puts a name to the unnamed "king of Assyria."

Deportation by Sargon

It has been argued that, if it were not Shalmaneser who effected these changes, it was Sargon his successor, who did so, and that he was the unnamed "king of Assyria" of verse 24. It was Sargon who captured Samaria; whether he destroyed the city is not stated, he probably did not; but the city does not seem to be mentioned again after that date.

Sargon, however, was not the king who removed the entire nation of Israel from Palestine. He himself witnesses to this. He states that he removed *the inhabitants* of Samaria to Assyria, which is a very different matter: he gives the number of his captives as 27,280 persons, a goodly number considering the fighting and the length of the siege. His Inscription states:

"In the beginning of my reign the city of Samaria I besieged, I captured, ... 27,280 of its inhabitants I carried away."

It is therefore certain that Sargon did not remove the entire nation. He was not the king of Assyria who removed Israel out of God's sight, and he was not the one who brought in the mass of the Gentiles mentioned in verse 24.

Did Sargon bring in any aliens at all ? The Bible gives no answer to this question, but such was the invariable practice of the Assyrian conquerors. One of his inscriptions tells that he did bring in foreigners, and reads:

"The conqueror of the Thamudites, the Ibadidites, the Marsiminites and the Khapaijans, the remainder of whom was carried away, and whom he transported to the midst of the land of Beth-Omri."

This shows that he did so. How great this importation was does not transpire. Were they only enough to re-people the city of Samaria or more ?

On comparing the peoples here mentioned with those enumerated in II Kings xvii, 24, they do not appear to be the same peoples, which goes to confirm the conviction that it was not Sargon who imported the tribes mentioned in verse 24, for these came from Babylon, Cuthah, Ava, Hamath and Sepharvaim. These the king of Assyria "placed in the cities of Samaria, and they possessed Samaria and dwelt in the cities thereof." Note that "Samaria" here refers to the land and not to the city of Samaria.

At the time of the capture of Samaria the Jezreel prophecy of Hosea "I will cause to cease the kingdom of the house of Israel" was fulfilled. But his Lo-Ruhamah prophecy, "I will utterly take them away," was not yet fulfilled. Nor was Isaiah's Three Score and Five Years prophecy fulfilled : the fulfilment was due forty-five years from this date.

THE LAST ENTRY IN THE ISRAEL STATE RECORDS

The Official Records of the kingdom of Israel ceased with the fall of the kingdom. What was the last entry in the Records ? It was verse 5 of Chapter xvii. The words are:

> "And the king of Assyria came up throughout all the land, and went up to Samaria, and besieged it three years."

For reasons already given, all that follows was by another hand at a later date.

The statement in the Bible concerning the taking of the city is given in the next verse, and reads:

> "In the ninth year of Hoshea the king of Assyria took Samaria, and carried Israel away into Assyria, and placed them in Hala, and in Habor by the river Gozan, and in the cities of the Medes."

The words "and in the cities of the Medes" are important as indicating the time when these words were written. They prove that this verse was not written at the time of the fall of Samaria in 721, but at earliest several years afterwards. The captives were not at once put into the cities of the Medes, for the simple reason that Media in 721 did not belong to the Assyrians, but they were moved thither after Sargon had invaded and conquered Media. These words were probably written long years afterwards by Ezra.

The verses subsequent to this verse 6 do not continue a narrative: they do not tell the story following the fall of Samaria: they are not a history of that period: they proceed to give a review or summary of the whole history of the Ten Tribed kingdom, telling of the sad declension of Israel from the Worship and Laws of Jehovah. They do not read like a record made at the time of the fall of Samaria, but like those of a commentator of a much later period. They review, from a religious standpoint, the Kingdom and the end of the kingdom-less People.

This Review ends in the following words:

> "Therefore the Lord was very angry with Israel, and removed them out of His sight : there was none left but the tribe of Judah only.
> Also Judah kept not the commandments of the Lord their God, but walked in the statutes of Israel which they made. And the Lord rejected all the seed of Israel, and afflicted them, and delivered them into the hands of spoilers, until He had cast them out of His sight, as He said by all His servants the prophets. So was Israel carried away out of their own land to Assyria unto this day" (II Kings xvii, 18-23).

This is a most important statement. Four points at least call for special notice.

(1) The expression removed "out of His sight" is considered, in the case of God's chosen people, to mean being cast out of the Holy Land on which the eyes of the Almighty ever rested.

> "A land which the Lord thy God careth for: the eyes of the Lord thy God are always upon it, from the beginning of the year even unto the end of the year" (Deut. xi, 12).

This same expression concerning Israel is used by Jeremiah as a warning to the house of Judah.

25

"But go ye now unto My place which was in Shiloh, where I set My name at the first, and see what I did to it for the wickedness of My people Israel. . . . Therefore will I do unto this house, which is called by My name, wherein ye trust, and unto the place which I gave to you and to your fathers, as I have to Shiloh. And I will cast you out of My sight, as I have cast out all your brethren, even the whole seed of Ephraim" (Jer. vii, 12-15).

(2) It is quite clear that these words were *not* written upon the fall of Samaria because of what is said about Judah, that "Judah kept not the commandments of the Lord their God." This we recognise was no true description of Judah at the period under consideration. Hezekiah was king of Judah at the time, and in no reign did Judah so steadfastly keep the commandments of God. Nor was it true in the days of Josiah, but it was a very true description of Judah after the death of Josiah. Hence this statement was made long years after 721. The whole statement points to its being the work of Ezra.

(3) The words, "So was Israel carried away out of their own land to Assyria *unto this day*," also makes it certain that this account was not written upon the fall of Samaria, for the simple reason that Israel was not all carried away in 721, for we read of a remnant in the land as late as the time of Josiah. Therefore it could only have been true after the days of that king. This again points to the period of Ezra.

(4) From this passage it is evident that between the reign of Josiah and the time of this statement the entire Israel population had been cast out of their own land. The words admit of no alternative.

"the Lord . . . removed them out of His sight" . . .
"until He had cast them out of His sight" . . .
"Until the Lord removed Israel out of His sight" . . .

and to leave no doubt as to the meaning:

"there was none left but the tribe of Judah only."

Surely this is conclusive and final.

Who should know the situation better than Ezra? In the face of this emphatic pronouncement any present-day opinions are valueless.

Our knowledge of the Israelites in the land after the fall of their kingdom is at best but scanty. With the extinction of the kingdom there was an end of all State records ; the government and rule had passed into Assyrian hands, and there was no one in Israel to write the history of the tributary people. It can only be gained either from the records of the kingdom of Judah or from secular history of the epoch.

The kingdom of Judah continued to exist for a hundred and thirty-three years after the downfall of the kingdom of Israel. During those long years Judah's State Records were carefully kept, until this kingdom in turn was destroyed in 587 B.C.. It is in these records that we may expect to find, as we actually do, occasional allusions to Israel still in the land of Samaria, which it must be remembered had then become a portion of the Assyrian empire. Such allusions are only made in so far as they concerned the Judah kingdom, they are scanty enough and in no way purport to be a history of Israel.

There are at least three such references in the Bible:

(1) The first is one concerning the siege and fall of Samaria, mentioned in II Kings xviii, 9 to 12, where we are informed that the siege began in the fourth year of Hezekiah's reign, and that the city was captured in his sixth year: and further that the captives were transported to Assyria.

(2) A second reference is cited by Dr. Dimont from II Chronicles xxx and xxxi as evidence that after the fall of Samaria there were many Israelites left in their land after the deportation by Sargon. These chapters give an account of the great Passover held in Jerusalem by Hezekiah, to which he invited the Israelites, most of whom rejected the invitation with scorn, while very many accepted and attended the Feast.

This so-called "evidence" is examined further on.

(3) A third allusion is made to the remnant of Israel still found in the land of Samaria in the reign of Josiah, recorded in II Chronicles xxxiv. This tells of the religious revival brought about by this godly young king of Judah, and of a Passover he subsequently held, to which he invited the remnant of Israel, who responded and attended the feast. This is proof that there were some Israelites in their own land in the time of Josiah.

27

This king not only purged Judah of her heathen altars, groves, high places and molten and carved images, but he did the same work in the land of Samaria, territory under Assyrian rule. It seems amazing that a king of Judah was permitted to do so. The Assyrian governor probably cared little what was done in religious matters so long as it did not affect his government and tribute.

It is clear from the Scriptures that there were Israelites in their own land long after the fall of their kingdom, all of which is in strict accord with the prophecies.

This concludes our study of the Invasions and Deportations as recorded in the Scriptures.

There is yet another invasion and deportation to be considered which is not fully told in the Bible.

CHAPTER IV

THE FOURTH INVASION

CONTENTS

The Fourth Invasion.
> By Esar-Haddon, son of Sennacherib.
> Date 676 B.C.
> No King in Israel.

Palestine Invaded.
> Invasion and Conquest of Judah.
> (A Previous Invasion of Judah).
> Manasseh, King of Judah taken Prisoner.
> Later Released and Reinstated.
> No Captives of Judah Carried Away.

Israelites Removed from The Land of Samaria.

Aliens Imported into the Land of Samaria.
> "Instead of Israel."
> Enumeration of the Imported Aliens.

Isaiah's Three Score and Five Years' Prophecy. Fulfilled.
> Israel no longer "a People."

Hosea's Lo-Ruhamah Prophecy. Fulfilled.
> "I will utterly take them away."

Josiah's Reform in the Land of Israel.

Table of the Invasions and Deportations of Israel.

CHAPTER IV

THE FOURTH INVASION

This Fourth Invasion is not given in the Second Book of
Kings. It is briefly told in the Second Book of Chronicles, which,
as already stated, deals only with the history of Judah. The
Bible does not definitely tell us of the effect it had upon Israel.
The Israelites naturally could give no account of it themselves.

ESAR-HADDON'S INVASION OF PALESTINE

The invading king was Esar-Haddon. Though his name is
not given in the Scripture narrative we know from Assyrian
inscriptions that he was the emperor who made the invasion,
which can be read in the Encyclopaedia Brittanica.

This invasion of Palestine was but a part in the great campaign. It took place about B.C. 676, a time when the Israel
nation had no king of their own, in fact, it was forty-five years
after the fall of Samaria when the kingdom ceased. During
these years Israel had been ruled by an Assyrian governor.

It may hardly be correct to speak of it as an invasion of
Israel. It was really an invasion of Judah, who had hitherto
withstood the efforts of Assyria to subdue her.

A PREVIOUS INVASION OF JUDAH

It will be remembered that Sennacherib, some seven years
after the fall of Samaria, had made a great effort to conquer the
Jewish kingdom, but Judah at the last moment was saved by
the direct interposition of God. For though Sennacherib devas-
tated Judea, took fenced cities and carried away a great host
of captives, yet he was not able to capture Jerusalem. He was
compelled to retire to Assyria with a depleted army that had
well nigh been annihilated by a devastating plague, thus was

30

Judah delivered out of the hand of Assyria, and her territory remained intact.

The Sennacherib inscriptions assert that he took forty-six fenced cities and removed some 200,150 captives, whom he placed in the same regions whither the captives of Israel had all been transported by previous emperors. Thus to the captives of Israel were added a great number from the tribes of Judah and Benjamin and of the Levites.

Esar-Haddon, however, now succeeded in doing what his father had failed to do. He conquered Judea, and took Manasseh its king captive and sent him away a prisoner in chains to Babylon. The brief narrative is in II Chronicles xxxiii, 11.

> "Wherefore the Lord brought upon them the captains of the host of the king of Assyria, which took Manasseh among the thorns, and bound him with fetters, and carried him to Babylon" (II Chronicles xxxiii, 11).

Here again we have another verse that speaks of a "King of Assyria" without the mention of his name. But from secular history we know that it was Esar-Haddon.

In his captivity Manasseh repented of his evil ways and turned to the God of ISRAEL, and later he was released and reinstated once more as king of Judah, and the kingdom continued till its destruction in 587 B.C. by Nebuchadnezzar.

There is no explanation why Judah was not annexed by Esar-Haddon. Further it would appear that no Jewish captives were deported.

GENTILES SETTLED IN THE LAND OF SAMARIA

It was after this campaign that Esar-Haddon brought in foreigners into the land of Samaria, which hitherto had been occupied by Israel. In accord with the accepted policy of the Assyrian kings Esar-Haddon removed the Israelites, and into their emptied land made a wholesale importation of Gentiles.

These various alien tribes were in time blended into one people in the land, and were therefore called Samaritans. They themselves, as we shall see later on, made no claim whatever to be Israelites; they openly confessed that they were foreigners, who had been forcibly settled in that land, and this by Esar-

31

Haddon. Some years later there were still other Gentiles brought in by Asnapper (Ezra iv, 10). This last king is identified with Assurbani-pul, the son of Esar-Haddon.

The great influx of Gentiles was after this Fourth invasion and recorded in II Kings xvii, 24.

"And the king of Assyria brought men from Babylon, and from Cuthah, and from Ava, and from Hamath, and from Sepharvaim, and placed them in the cities of Samaria instead of the children of Israel: and they possessed Samaria, and dwelt in the cities thereof" (II Kings xvii, 24).

We have already seen that this unnamed "king of Assyria" could not have been Shalmaneser or Sargon, and that he must have been Esar-Haddon. The statement that they were placed in the cities of Samaria "instead of Israel" implies a great deportation of Israelites, and that Israel was no longer "a People" in Palestine.

FULFILMENT OF TWO PROPHECIES

Two prophecies ran out at this time:

(1) Isaiah's prophecy of The Three Score and Five Years: "shall Ephraim be broken, that it be not a people."

(2) Hosea's Lo-Ruhamah prophecy: "I will utterly take them away."

And yet, even after this wholesale removal of the Israel population, there were still some Israelites left behind, because we read of some being present there in the reign of Josiah, who reigned in Judah some years after Esar-Haddon's invasion.

But Jeremiah who wrote at a later time stated that in his day Israel had been removed out of God's sight, "even the whole seed of Ephraim" (Jeremiah vii, 15).

The Table No. I gives an analysis of these invasions.

TABLE No. I

ANALYSIS OF THE INVASIONS

<u>THE FIRST INVASION.</u>   Unimportant.

> The Kingdom Intact : No Territory Annexed.
> No Captives Carried Away.
> Heavy Financial Loss.

<u>THE SECOND INVASION.</u>   Very serious.

> The Kingdom Reduced
> (1) In Territory :
>> (*a*) Most of Galilee Lost ;
>> (*b*) All Transjordania Lost.
>> Kingdom reduced by $\frac{2}{3}$ in size.
>
> (2) In Population :
>> (*a*) Captives from most of Galilee ;
>> (*b*) Captives of all Transjordania.

<u>THE THIRD INVASION.</u>   Most Important.

> The End of the Kingdom.
> The Whole Land Annexed.
> A Very Small Deportation.
> The People Remain in the Land.

<u>THE FOURTH INVASION.</u>   Most Important.

> The Whole Nation Carried Away.
> No longer a People.
> Only Judah left in Palestine.

Bearing in mind this removal of the nation and its replacement by imported Gentiles, attention must be drawn to the reforms undertaken there by Josiah. It has already been noted that this godly young king of Judah not only purged Judea of idolatry, but that he carried this work into the land of Samaria, the old home of the Israelites, which was then Assyrian territory. People usually think of Josiah doing this task amongst the Israelites. But was this really so? Was it not also amongst the new comers into the land, amongst the mass of the new population of the heathens? These new Samaritans all worshipped their various racial gods and at the same time sacrificed to "the God of the land," the God of ISRAEL. At the beginning of their dwelling there they feared not the Lord; but when they were plagued by lions, they requested the king of Assyria, who had placed them there, to send them a priest from among the captives of Israel to teach them "the manner of the God of the land" (II Kings xvii, 25 and onwards). So they worshipped their own gods and sacrificed to the God of ISRAEL. This was the very plea that they urged upon Ezra in later years (Ezra iv, 2). It was amongst this people that Josiah carried out the work of breaking down their images, altars and shrines, and also of course the heathen altars that Israel had previously set up.

The following Table gives at a glance the Invasions and Deportations of Israel by Assyria.

TABLE No. II

ASSYRIAN INVASIONS AND DEPORTATIONS OF ISRAEL

Invasion	Date	Assyrian Emperor	King of Israel	King of Judah	References
First		(Pul) Tiglath-pileser	Menahem	Azariah	II Kings xv, 19-20
Second	741	(Pul) Tiglath-pileser	Pekah	Ahaz	II Kings xv, 29 I Chron. v, 26
Third	721	Shalmaneser (Sargon)	Hoshea	Hezekiah	II Kings xvii, 3 (Hosea i, 4)
Fourth	676	Esar-Haddon	No King	Manasseh	II Chron. xxxiii, 11 (Hosea i, 6) (Ezra iv, 2)

Isaiah's Sixty-Five Years

EXAMINATION OF CONTRARY VIEWS

CONTENTS

Denial 1. That Israel was ever Lost.

  2. That Israel was Completely Carried away.

Maintained by Dr. H. L. Goudge, Regius Professor of Divinity in the University of Oxford.

  By Dr. C. T. Dimont, Principal of the Theological College, Salisbury.

Dr. Dimont's Reasons for this Denial.

  1. Because Contrary to the Scriptures.

  2. Because Contrary to the Monuments.

Causes of Error in these Reasonings.

  1. All the Scripture Evidence not Adduced.

  2. All the Historical Evidence not Considered.

  3. Thinking a Description of one Period must be True of another much Later Period.

  4. Not realising that the Situation at one Time might change with the Lapse of Years.

  Hence Wrong Conclusions Inevitable.

Every Statement was True at the Time when it was Written.

A Review of all the Evidence.

  The Ten Tribes wholly Removed from Palestine.

Date of Hezekiah's Passover.

Table No. III, The Reign of Hoshea in Hezekiah's Early Days.

EXAMINATION OF CONTRARY VIEWS

We are now in a position to examine the arguments of those who deny that the Bible gives any countenance to the idea that the nation of Israel was wholly removed out of Palestine.

The *final* statement of the Scriptures on this point is:

> "Therefore the Lord was very angry with Israel, and moved them out of His sight: there was none left but the tribe of Judah only. . . . So was Israel carried away out of their own land unto this day" (II Kings xvii, 18-23).

Dr. H. L. Goudge, Regius Professor of Divinity in the University of Oxford, in his booklet entitled, "The British Israel Theory" on page 88 writes, "First, there is not a particle of evidence that there were ever any lost tribes in the British Israelite sense."

This is an amazing statement; it is not documented and no proof either from Scripture or Assyrian inscriptions is given in support of the assertion, which precludes detailed examination. Suffice it to say that the term "lost" in reference to Israel is found in the marginal reading of Isaiah xvii, 13, in the Revised Version.

Dr. C. T. Dimont, Principal of Salisbury Theological College, and Chancellor of the Diocese, says that there were no lost tribes; that all the Israelites were not carried away into Assyria; that only some twenty thousand odd in all were removed, a negligible number of the population of Israel. Here are his exact words: In his pamphlet "The Legend of British Israel," on page 5 he writes:

> "The British cannot be the descendants of the Lost Ten Tribes because no such body of lost tribes exists or ever

existed. The assertion that all the Ten Northern Tribes were carried away to Assyria is contrary to Scripture and to the testimony of the monuments. Sargon, the king of Assyria, says that he carried away from Israel 27,290 captives."

He states here that the complete deportation of the nation is contrary
       (1) to the Scriptures, and
       (2) to the Monuments.

He then proceeds to give his evidence, which needs our careful examination.

THE TESTIMONY OF THE MONUMENTS

Only one single monument is appealed to, that of Sargon; while others are ignored.

The denial of the wholesale deportation is based on the inscription, which has been already quoted above:

"In the beginning of my reign the city of Samaria I besieged, I captured, . . . 27,280 of its inhabitants I carried away . . ."

Dr. Dimont insists that this proves that the whole nation was never entirely removed. This one inscription is apparently sufficient to disprove the statement of the Word of God. The *final* statement on the subject in the Bible is set aside in favour of the inscription of a heathen king. Would it surprise Dr. Dimont to learn that both these statements were absolutely correct?

THE TESTIMONY OF THE SCRIPTURES

Dr. Dimont adduces two passages of Scripture to prove that the whole nation was never carried away. He, however, wholly ignores at least one important one that refutes his contention, a proceeding which renders void his conclusions; the most important evidence from Scripture is not produced.

With regard to the subject of Scripture Evidence, it ought not to be necessary to point out that statements of fact apply, unless otherwise clearly stated, only to the time in which they were uttered or written, and that they do not necessarily describe the position of affairs of a much later date.

Few will hold that all the Ten Tribes were carried away at the time of Sargon, because, as Dr. Dimont points out, the wholesale transportation of Israel in 721 B.C. is contrary to Scripture, because there were Israelites still in their land in the reigns of Hezekiah and of Josiah. But he ignores statements in later Scriptures describing later conditions. There can be no real contradiction in these various statements; they were made at different times, and each was absolutely true at the time it was made.

Dr. Dimont contents himself with these two statements made concerning Israel, and no other. But surely the whole of the evidence should be considered before pronouncing a verdict.

The whole crux of the question turns upon the fixing of dates.

(1) Samaria fell in 721 B.C., and there were Israelites left in the land at that time. There is no doubt that Sargon's testimony that he only removed 27,280 was perfectly true.

(2) There were Israelites still in the land in the reign of Hezekiah king of Judah, who reigned from 726 to 697 B.C.

(3) Some Israelites were still found there at a later period, in the time of Josiah, who began to reign in 677 B.C. This is the last information given about Israel in the Judah records.

(4) What was the date of the statement that tells of Israel's being utterly carried away into Assyria out of God's sight, and that only Judah remained behind?

"So was Israel carried away out of their own land unto this day." What date was "this day"? The date of its writing was the time of Ezra. The earliest possible date 561 B.C., the latest being 536 B.C., the time of Judah's captivity in Babylon.

It should be remembered that there was a considerable lapse of time between the fall of Samaria and the days of Ezra, about two hundred years. A good many things could have happened, and certainly one event of great importance did happen, in that period, though there was no historian in Israel to record the happenings.

Dr. Dimont cannot be ignorant that the invasion of Israel by Shalmaneser and Sargon was not the last invasion of the Holy Land by Assyria. He cannot have forgotten that there was a great invasion of Palestine by the emperor Esar-Haddon, about 676 B.C. as testified by the Monuments. Anybody can read about it in the *Encyclopædia Britannica*. Yet he entirely ignores this testimony as if it had no bearing on the question under consideration, and his readers are sorely misled. Surely all the relevant evidence should be adduced to arrive at a right conclusion.

Events had occurred which made the state of affairs very different from what they were in the bygone days of Sargon and his inscription ; and different from what obtained in the days of Hezekiah.

The Bible gives no direct account of Esar-Haddon's invasion as far as Israel was concerned, but the history of Judah tells of it, because the campaign sorely affected the kingdom of Judah (II Chron. xxxiii, 11).

The Bible also at a much later date refers back to this invasion, and shows how it affected Israel (Ezra iv, 2).

It is strange that anyone should think that the state of affairs which existed in 721 B.C., and which then was correctly described, must remain unaltered by the changes during the stirring times of the ensuing century. Was no change possible or probable ? Changes did take place which made the statement "so was Israel carried away out of their own land to Assyria unto this day" absolutely true.

Esar-Haddon effected a radical change in population of the land of Israel, he removed Israel and replaced them by Gentiles. This filling the land with foreigners is referred to in Ezra iv, 2.

> "Now when the adversaries of Judah and Benjamin heard that the children of the captivity builded the temple of the Lord God of ISRAEL, then they came to Zerubbabel and to the chief of the fathers, and said unto them, Let us build with you: for we seek your God as ye do, and we do sacrifice unto Him since the days of Esar-Haddon, king of Assur, which brought us up hither."

Two points need consideration here:

(1) These Samaritans did not claim that they were Israelites.

(2) They definitely stated that they were foreigners, the peoples whom the Assyrians had brought into the land in the reign of Esar-Haddon. They tell us emphatically who they were and by whom they were imported thither. They do not

mention Shalmaneser or Sargon as having done so. It is clear therefore that the wholesale importation of Samaritans was *at the time of* and *by* Esar-Haddon. There were no Israelites there at that time, but only these imported Gentiles, whom the Jews always regarded as such, and with whom they would have no dealing. The Jews would never have rejected these advances so contemptuously had they been made by Israelites.

It was the invariable practice and policy of the Assyrian monarchs to remove conquered peoples wholesale from their conquered lands and settle them in the distant parts of the empire, and to repopulate the evacuated lands with folk from other districts. A policy which led eventually to the undoing of that empire.

The Gentile tribes imported into Samaria were those who are mentioned in II Kings xvii, 24.

But even at this period Esar-Haddon had not removed the last vestige of Israel, for some were still found in the land in the reign of Josiah, who was king of Judah some years after this invasion.

The statement made by Jeremiah, which has already been quoted above, has a bearing on the deportation of Israel from Palestine. It was written after the days of Josiah, before the final destruction of Jerusalem by Nebuchadnezzar. How did he regard the position of Israel at that time? Speaking to Judah, he gave God's message thus:

> "And I will cast you out of My sight as I have cast out *all* your brethren, even the *whole* seed of Ephraim" (Jer. vii, 15).

The words "I have cast out all your brethren" points to a complete removal of Israel from their land ; and this is emphasised by the added words, "even the whole seed of Ephraim." Hence even before the Jewish captivity to Babylon there were no Israelites left, the whole nation had been carried away.

Here it may be objected, how could this remnant of Israel living in their own land in the days of Josiah have been removed into Assyria so as to make Jeremiah's statement a true word. Who could have effected it and when? The Bible

41

gives no direct answer: but it does tell us that Asnapper, king of Assyria (identified with Assurbani-pul, son of Esar-Haddon) who reigned after the time of Josiah, did bring into Israel's land several Gentile tribes as recorded in Ezra iv, 9-10. If he followed the traditional Assyrian policy, he must have located them in places from which he evacuated the Israel remnant. Here at least was a fitting opportunity for the complete removal of any remnant of Israel.

Thus there are three recorded Importations of Gentiles with corresponding Deportations of Israel into and from the land of Israel.

1. By Sargon in 721 to replenish the Israelites whom he removed from Samaria.

2. The mass importation by Esar-Haddon in 676.

3. By Asnapper after Josiah's time.

REVIEW OF THE EVIDENCE

To summarise:

(1) Sargon's statement was quite truthful, and is exactly what happened at that time. It in no way contradicts the truth of the later Bible statement made concerning a subsequent time.

(2) The fact that there were many Israelites in their land in the reign of Hezekiah is correct. It in no way contradicts the truth of the Bible statement made at a later date concerning a much later period, and it accords with prophecies on the subject.

(3) The fact that there were some Israelites in the land in the days of Josiah is perfectly true, but it does not necessarily contradict the truth of a later Bible statement concerning a later date.

(4) The statement of Jeremiah only confirms the *final* pronouncement of the Bible on the subject.

(5) The statement of the Samaritans to the returned captives of Judah also entirely corroborates the *final* word of the Bible as to the complete removal of the whole nation from Palestine.

Thus the evidence put forward by Dr. Dimont from the Monuments and from the Scriptures, when examined, is found to be no evidence at all against the fact that Israel was wholly removed from their land, but is rather in complete accord with the Bible statement.

THE DATE OF HEZEKIAH'S PASSOVER

THE DATE OF HEZEKIAH'S PASSOVER

One point more about the Scripture evidence given by Dr. Dimont. He says that the presence of the great number of Israelites at the great Passover held by King Hezekiah in Jerusalem is proof that Israel was never entirely carried away to Assyria upon the fall of Samaria.

Surely, Dr. Dimont must know that this incident has no bearing on the point. He must know that this Passover took place *before* the invasion of Israel by Shalmaneser, and still more years before the capture of Samaria by Sargon, and not after it.

The ordinary reader may be pardoned for thinking that this Passover was held after the downfall of the kingdom of Israel, because the reign of Hezekiah in the Bible is given after the reign of Hoshea. The observations made in Chapter I on the difficulties of editing two separate histories into one is here exemplified. The universal mistake of thus misdating the Passover is explainable. As a matter of fact, the early events of Hezekiah's reign took place in the reign of Hoshea. These two kings for several years were reigning at the same time, one in Judah and the other in Israel. The celebration of the Passover took place in the first year of Hezekiah, at which time Hoshea was reigning in Israel, and it was five years before the conquest of Israel. The presence of many Israelites at the feast therefore has nothing whatever to do with the situation of affairs after the fall of Samaria, and is no proof that the whole nation was not carried away.

That there were many Israelites in the land is a fact, but not on the evidence adduced by Dr. Dimont.

The following Table, No. III, makes the position clear.

THE REIGN OF HOSHEA IN THE EARLY DAYS OF HEZEKIAH

King of Israel	King of Judah	
Pekah	Ahaz	Invasion of Israel by Tiglath-pileser.
Hoshea 1 year of reign		
2		
3	—**Hezekiah**—— 1 year of reign	Temple cleansed. Great Passover.
4		
	2	
5		
	3	
6		
	4	
7		Invasion of Israel by Shalmaneser.
	5	
8		
	6	
721 9		Fall of Samaria by Sargon, 721 B.C.
	7	
	8	
No King		
	9	

44

CHAPTER VI

THE IMPORTED GENTILES

There are three distinct records of the importation of foreigners into the emptied land of Israel.

Two of these are found in the Bible, while the other is recorded in the Assyrian inscription of Sargon.

That there were more such importations is not denied, because of what we know of the policy of the Assyrian conquests, but they are not recorded as far as can be discovered. For instance, no one doubts that, after Tiglath-pileser carried away the Israelites from the extreme north and from Transjordania, he filled up the depopulated territory with peoples from distant regions as was the custom of Assyria: but this is not recorded.

The records of the three importations of aliens give a list of the nations or tribes thus brought in and settled in the land of Israel.

In passing, it may be stated here that, in the case of the deportations of the Jews later by the Babylonians under Nebuchadnezzar, the depopulated land of Judea was never colonised by aliens, but remained empty till the return of some of the Jews after seventy years captivity in Babylon.

The First and earliest of the three Groups is that which Sargon brought in after his capture of Samaria and the downfall of the kingdom of Israel in 721. As said above this list is not recorded in the Bible.

The Second Group, which was by far the largest, was made by Esar-Haddon in 676, and the list of those nations so imported is that recorded in II Kings xvii, 24.

The Third Group was brought in later by Asnapper, the son of Esar-Haddon, and the list of these newcomers is given in Ezra iv, 9.

For comparison the component nations of each Group are given in the following Table No. IV.

TABLE NO. IV
THE IMPORTED GENTILES

First Group By Sargon	Second Group By Esar-Haddon	Third Group By Asnapper
Thamudites Ibadidites Marsiminites Khapayans	Men of Babylon Cuthah Ava Hamath Sepharvaim	Dinaites Apharsathchites Tarpelites Aphrasites Archevites Babylonians Susanchites Dehavites Elamites

The three Groups are quite distinct from one another: each represents groups of different nations. There was an interval of about forty-five years between Groups I and II, and several years between Groups II and III.

None of these Groups consisted wholly of one single nation. Each consisted of mixed peoples gathered from different regions. They were not a homogeneous crowd.

Further a Group did not consist of peoples of one religion; they did not all worship the same god, but gods many and lords many. This may be gathered from II Kings xvii, 30 and 31, where each nation had its own special object of worship.

The nations of one Group thus brought together were from a political, social and religious point of view very different. It took years for them all to become fused into a single united race in the land as we find them in the time of our Lord.

Under such conditions they were powerless to combine or rebel against the suzereign power. Herein appears the astuteness of the Assyrian policy.

On the other hand all accounts of the deported Israelites tell of their settlement (at first at least) in one single large

46

region, Hala, Habor, Hara and the river Gozan; a fact which may be considered rather strange.

It was here that Tiglath-pileser placed the first captives of Israel in 741 B.C. It was here that Sargon brought the inhabitants of captured Samaria. But be it noted that, true to Assyrian policy, a few years later he broke up the unity of these captives by removing very many of them into the "cities of the Medes," whom he had then conquered. Esar-Haddon moved Israel "into Assyria," presumably to the same regions as the previous captives, though the exact locality is not mentioned. We do not know what Asnapper did. All we know was that there were some Israelites in their land after Esar-Haddon's time, and that his son brought Group III into the land; further that at a still later date, before the destruction of Jerusalem by Nebuchadnezzar, Jeremiah tells us that Israel, even the whole house of Ephraim, had been cast out of the land. The natural conclusion is that Asnapper had removed this remnant before he imported the Gentiles of Group III. Ezra is clear that none of the chosen race was left in Palestine save Judah.

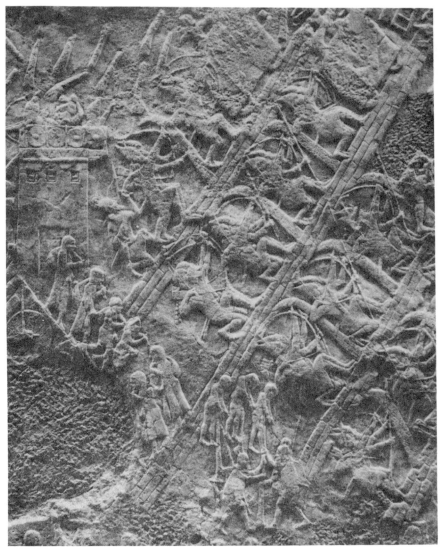

The siege of Lachish: *Sennacherib, 704–681 B.C.*

British Museum
Lachish Room

48